Pebble™ Plus

Mighty Machines
Rescue Boats

by Carol K. Lindeen

Consulting Editor: Gail Saunders-Smith, PhD

Capstone
press

Mankato, Minnesota

Pebble Plus is published by Capstone Press,
151 Good Counsel Drive, P.O. Box 669, Mankato, Minnesota 56002.
www.capstonepress.com

1 2 3 4 5 6 10 09 08 07 06 05

Library of Congress Cataloging-in-Publication Data
Lindeen, Carol K., 1976–
Rescue boats / by Carol K. Lindeen.
p. cm.—(Pebble plus: mighty machines)
Includes bibliographical references and index.
ISBN 0-7368-3655-1 (hardcover)
1. Search and rescue boats—Juvenile literature. 2. Lifeboats—Juvenile literature.
I. Title. II. Series.
VM466.S4L55 2005
623.826—dc22   2004015105

Summary: Simple text and photographs present rescue boats, their parts, and how people use rescue boats.

Editorial Credits
Mari C. Schuh, editor; Molly Nei, set designer; Kate Opseth and Ted Williams, book designers;
   Jo Miller, photo researcher; Scott Thoms, photo editor

Photo Credits
Check Six 2004/Barry Smith, 1, 17
Corbis/Cordaiy Photo Library Ltd./John Framar, 6–7; James Marshall, 18–19; Neil Rebinowitz, 21
Corbis Saba/Najlah Feanny, 13
DVIC/PHC Gloria Montgomery, 5; SSGT Michael Buytas, 14–15
Photo Network/Mary Messenger, 10–11
Unicorn Stock Photos/Dede Gilman, 9
U.S. Coast Guard Photo/PA3 Anthony Juarez, cover

Note to Parents and Teachers

The Mighty Machines set supports national standards related to science, technology, and society. This book describes and illustrates rescue boats. The images support early readers in understanding the text. The repetition of words and phrases helps early readers learn new words. This book also introduces early readers to subject-specific vocabulary words, which are defined in the Glossary section. Early readers may need assistance to read some words and to use the Table of Contents, Glossary, Read More, Internet Sites, and Index sections of the book.

Table of Contents

What Are Rescue Boats?

Rescue boats help people
in danger on oceans,
big lakes, and rivers.

Parts and Gear

Rescue boats have antennas.
Antennas help rescue crews
find boats in trouble.

antennas

Rescue boats have strong ropes. The crew uses ropes to tow boats to safety.

rope

Rescue workers wear life jackets to stay safe. Rescue boats have extra life jackets for the people they rescue.

To the Rescue

A rescue boat gets a call.

Another boat is broken

and is sinking.

13

The crew rushes

onto the rescue boat.

They get ready

for the rescue.

A crew member steers
the rescue boat.
The rescue boat speeds
over big waves.

The rescue crew finds the
people who need help.
The rescue boat carries
everyone safely to shore.

Rescue crews use

rescue boats to help people

in emergencies.

Glossary

antenna—a tall wire that receives radio signals

crew—a group of people who work together

emergency—a sudden and dangerous situation; people need to deal with emergencies quickly.

life jacket—a vest that floats; people wear life jackets to stay safe in boats and in water; life jackets help people float in water.

steer—to make a boat or car go in a certain direction

tow—to pull along behind; a rescue boat can tow another boat that is broken or damaged.

Read More

Ethan, Eric. *Rescue Boats.* Emergency Vehicles. Milwaukee: Gareth Stevens, 2002.

Oxlade, Chris. *Emergency Vehicles.* Transportation around the World. Chicago: Heinemann Library, 2001.

Internet Sites

FactHound offers a safe, fun way to find Internet sites related to this book. All of the sites on FactHound have been researched by our staff.

Here's how:

1. Visit *www.facthound.com*

2. Type in this special code **0736836551** for age-appropriate sites. Or enter a search word related to this book for a more general search.

3. Click on the **Fetch It** button.

FactHound will fetch the best sites for you!

Index

Word Count: 124
Grade: 1
Early-Intervention Level: 14